SHOSHONE

Big Buddy Books
An Imprint of Abdo Publishing
abdopublishing.com

Katie Lajiness

abdopublishing.com

Published by Abdo Publishing, a division of ABDO, PO Box 398166, Minneapolis, Minnesota 55439.
Copyright © 2017 by Abdo Consulting Group, Inc. International copyrights reserved in all countries. No part
of this book may be reproduced in any form without written permission from the publisher. Big Buddy Books™
is a trademark and logo of Abdo Publishing.

Printed in the United States of America, North Mankato, Minnesota.
062016
092016

THIS BOOK CONTAINS
RECYCLED MATERIALS

Cover Photo: © Luc Novovitch/Alamy; Shutterstock.com.
Interior Photos: © AS400 DB/Corbis (p. 27); © David R. Frazier Photolibrary, Inc./Alamy (p. 16); © INTERFOTO/
    Alamy (p. 30); © iStockphoto.com (pp. 21, 23); © NativeStock.com/AngelWynn (pp. 5, 9, 11, 17, 19, 26);
    © NativeStock/North Wind Picture Archives (p. 15); © Luc Novovitch/Alamy (p. 29); Shutterstock.com (p. 11);
    © Ted Streshinsky/Corbis (p. 25); © Don Troiani/Corbis (13).

Coordinating Series Editor: Tamara L. Britton
Graphic Design: Adam Craven

Library of Congress Cataloging-in-Publication Data
Lajiness, Katie, author.
  Shoshone / Katie Lajiness.
Minneapolis, MN : ABDO Publishing Company, 2017. | Series:
  Native Americans
LCCN 2015050496 | ISBN 9781680782028 (print) | ISBN 9781680774979 (ebook)
Shoshoni Indians--History--Juvenile literature. | Shoshoni
  Indians--Social life and customs--Juvenile literature.
LCC E99.S4 L35 2017 | DDC 978.004/974574--dc23
LC record available at http://lccn.loc.gov/2015050496

CONTENTS

Amazing People

Hundreds of years ago, North America was mostly wild, open land. Native American tribes lived on the land. They had their own languages and **customs**.

The Shoshone (shuh-SHOHN) are one Native American tribe. They are known for their hunting skills and beautiful clothing. Let's learn more about these Native Americans.

Did You Know?

The name *Shoshone* means "plentiful grass."

Shoshone families take part in festivals to honor their native customs.

SHOSHONE TERRITORY

Shoshone homelands were in what is now the western United States. There were three groups of Shoshone. They lived in present-day California, Idaho, Montana, Nevada, Oregon, Utah, and Wyoming. All Shoshone spoke the same language, but they practiced different **customs** and **traditions**.

CANADA

UNITED STATES

SHOSHONE HOMELANDS

OREGON

MONTANA

IDAHO

WYOMING

NEVADA

CALIFORNIA

UTAH

MEXICO

N
W · E
S

HOME LIFE

Some Shoshone families followed the animals they hunted. They built short-term homes called wickiups. These oval-shaped huts had a rough frame covered with plants and bark.

Other Shoshone did not move around as much. They lived in caves. By the 1700s, many began to build teepees wrapped in buffalo skin.

Today, Shoshone teepees are made out of fabric and painted with Native-American designs. Modern teepees are mostly used for ceremonies, and they are no longer used as homes.

What They Ate

The Shoshone ate a wide range of foods depending on where they lived. Some men hunted antelope, deer, rabbits, sheep, or squirrels. Others used fire to draw in salmon and then netted them. The Shoshone also caught grasshoppers to eat.

Shoshone women also provided food for their families. They made cakes from dried berries, nuts, and seeds. And, they cooked vegetables in pits beneath hot rocks.

Every autumn, many tribes came together to hunt buffalo.

Women collected pine nuts to grind into flour. They used the flour to make mush or bread.

Daily Life

The Shoshone lived in villages. Each community had a sweathouse. Spending time in the sweathouse helped keep them clean.

Shoshone tribes wore few clothes, especially during the warm months. As the weather grew colder, people put on animal furs and hides. Some Shoshone wore moccasins to keep their feet warm.

The best hunters dressed in deer and antelope skins. Many had **tattoos** on their faces and pierced ears. Skirts and hats were part of women's wardrobes.

Men often had long hair. Sometimes they wore feathers in their hair.

In a Shoshone village, people had different jobs. Men hunted for food. And, they traded furs for other goods.

Women took care of their homes. They sewed clothes made from animal skins. And, they made baskets. Children learned these skills from helping adults.

Shoshone women made pemmican cakes from animal fat, berries, deer meat, and seeds.

MADE BY HAND

The Shoshone made many objects by hand. They often used natural materials. These arts and crafts added beauty to everyday life.

Beadwork
Women placed beads in patterns to decorate items such as headdresses *(shown)*, moccasins, and dresses. Beads were made from glass, metal, or brass.

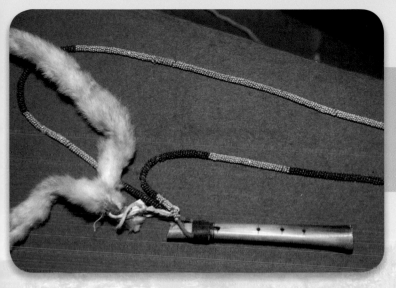

Bone Whistles

Shoshone eagle-bone whistles were used in many native ceremonies. They were made from an eagle's wing bone.

Games

Game pieces were carved from animal bone and then wrapped in leather.

Woven Baskets

Women wove baskets out of willow. They used the baskets to store items such as food.

Spirit Life

The Shoshone had many **spiritual** beliefs. Some believed the sun made the heavens and earth. Others thought Coyote and Wolf created their people.

All Shoshone tribes held dances and **ceremonies**. In 1870, the Shoshone and other tribes began holding Ghost Dances. They believed these ceremonies would bring their dead **ancestors** back to life.

Some Shoshone men wore tops known as *ghost shirts*. They believed these shirts would protect them from bullets and arrows.

STORYTELLERS

Stories are important to the Shoshone. Storytellers taught people about the tribe's **culture**, land, and history. The Shoshone told stories about animal characters such as Wolf and Coyote. Some stories were told through prayers, songs, and dances.

The Shoshone believed Wolf was a god. In many stories, Coyote does not like Wolf because the Shoshone respect Wolf.

FIGHTING FOR LAND

Throughout history, the Shoshone have struggled to keep their land. During the 1500s, European explorers arrived in Shoshone territory. American settlers came 300 years later.

Over time, the settlers began to push the Shoshone off their lands. In January 1863, the US Army attacked the Shoshone in what is now known as the Bear River **Massacre**. They killed 250 Shoshone men, women, and children.

Many Shoshone lived along Utah's Bear River. The area had plenty of animals to hunt and food to gather. Over time, many European settlers used this land to farm.

More white settlers moved onto tribal lands. In 1863, the first **treaty** of Fort Bridger reduced the size of the Shoshone's land in Utah.

During the 1930s, Shoshone fought to regain some of their rights. So, they formed their own tribal government.

In 2006, Shoshone tried to stop the US government from testing explosives. They believed the government's work was destroying their native land. After protests, the explosive tests were cancelled.

For decades, Shoshone families have worked to protect their tribal lands.

BACK IN TIME

c. 1700

The Northern and Eastern Shoshone received horses from European settlers. Tribes began hunting on horseback.

1782

Many Eastern Shoshone died from sicknesses brought over by European settlers.

c. 1500

The Shoshone began moving through what is now known as the Great Plains.

1804–1806

Sacagawea was the only Shoshone woman to join Meriwether Lewis and William Clark's group. The explorers mapped the American Northwest after the land was bought from France.

1968

The US government paid Shoshone for lands the government took from the tribe.

1900

Chief Washakie died. He was a wise man and a great fighter. Washakie was known for showing kindness to European settlers.

THE SHOSHONE TODAY

The Shoshone have a long, rich history. They are remembered for their native stories and meeting Lewis and Clark.

Shoshone roots run deep. Today, the people have kept alive those special things that make them Shoshone. Even though times have changed, many people carry the **traditions**, stories, and memories of the past into the present.

Did You Know?

In 2010, there were more than 7,800 Shoshone living in the United States.

Today, Shoshone children learn about their culture from powwows. The Shoshone Hannock Powwow includes rodeos, art shows, parades, and a feast.

"I fought to keep our land, our water, and our hunting grounds. Today, education is the weapon my people will need to protect them."

– Chief Washakie

GLOSSARY

ancestor a family member from an earlier time.

ceremony a formal event on a special occasion.

culture (KUHL-chuhr) the arts, beliefs, and ways of life of a group of people.

custom a practice that has been around a long time and is common to a group or a place.

massacre the violent and cruel killing of a large number of people.

spiritual (SPIHR-ih-chuh-wuhl) of or relating to the spirit or soul instead of physical things.

tattoo to mark the body with a picture or pattern by using a needle to put color under the skin.

tradition (truh-DIH-shuhn) a belief, a custom, or a story handed down from older people to younger people.

treaty an agreement made between two or more groups.

WEBSITES

To learn more about Native Americans, visit **booklinks.abdopublishing.com**. These links are routinely monitored and updated to provide the most current information available.

INDEX